Discipline Your Execution

Learn How To Beat Procrastination, Develop Self Discipline To Take Action and Start Achieving Your Big Goals!

Nicholas Mayor

Table of Contents:

Introduction 3
Chapter 1: Understanding the Biggest Obstacle To Execution.. 20
Chapter 2: Why Do People Procrastinate and Fail To Take Action? 28
Chapter 3: Change Your Mindset to Execute On Your Most Important Tasks 35
Chapter 4: Turn to Technology when Self-Control Fails 49
Chapter 5: Simplify Your Way to Action 53
Chapter 6: Crave Your Personal State of Flow ... 57
Chapter 7: Hold Yourself Accountable 62
Chapter 8: Don't Hesitate to Scale Things Up Once Things Get "Easy" 70
Chapter 9: Finish What You Start 72
Chapter 10: Embrace "the Art of Delaying" 75
Chapter 11: Bundle Your "Must Do's with Your "Should Do's" and "Want to Do's" 77
Chapter 12: Think Why You shouldn't Procrastinate and Rather Focus on Execution ... 81

Chapter 13: Reward Yourself after You Finish a Big Task 85

Chapter 14: Visualize Yourself Free from Procrastination 90

Chapter 15: Hang Out with Highly Motivated People Who Believe In Taking Action 94

Final Thoughts 102

Introduction

Let me tell you the story of my friend Bobby. Among our group of friends, Bobby had the most potential. Everybody knew it.

Anybody who knew Bobby knew that he was quick-witted, smart as a whip, and hard working. He was also great with people. He seemed to know the right things to say to the right people at the right time.

To say that Bobby had everything going for him would be an understatement indeed. It was very easy to think that in any group of friends, Bobby was the one going places.

With all that said, he did have one flaw. It didn't seem like much of a big deal back then, but come to think of it, this one character weakness proved to be his undoing. His flaw is that, if he did not like an assignment or a project, or feels unprepared, he would automatically put off on doing it.

Please understand that he wasn't lazy. It's not like he gets a project he doesn't like, and then he drops everything. Instead, he just drops that project and puts all his attention, effort and energy on other projects.

These are the things that he liked to do. These are the things that seemed more pleasurable to him. These are also things that he felt he could do easily.

Please understand that there's a big difference between being lazy and doing things the way Bobby did them. He just had this habit of kicking the can down the road regarding certain projects, decisions, and opportunities.

He keeps telling me of important projects he's working on. He knows that these are the very big things that would take his life to the next level. But every time I talk to him, it seems that the list never seems to change.

No matter how much time passes, he still has the same list. It's as if he was doing almost everything else, except for the things that truly mattered. My friend Bobby, for lack of a better word, is living far below his potential.

All his friends know that he could be making so much more money. They know that he could be so much more successful in his chosen field. But unfortunately, he seems stuck. That list of projects that he has is still there. It's as if nothing changed.

Please understand that regardless of how charismatic you are, and no matter how much you have going for you, if you procrastinate, you might end up like my friend Bobby. He works hard, he paid his dues, but unfortunately, life is not giving him the kind of rewards somebody with all his potential would otherwise deserve.

The Many Faces of Failure

It's easy to think that failure can only be defined one way. It's easy to think that failure just means total professional, relational, sexual, financial and physical disaster.

Well, failure can also be defined as knowing that you have what it takes to go far in life, but ending up going nowhere.

The truth is, people fail in many different ways. Most people are unable or unwilling to reach their fullest potential.

They know that they have what it takes. They know that there are opportunities that they come across that can lead to better outcomes. They know they are capable of so much more. And this is what makes certain types of failure so frustrating.

It's not like you are unable to get the good things in life. It's not like there's a massive wall of opposition standing in the way of you and the better things in life. But the problem is that you don't let it happen.

Now, don't get me wrong. I understand that there are many reasons why people fail. In fact, these reasons can be so specific that a hundred different people may have a hundred different reasons why they're not living up to their fullest potential.

This should not be a surprise. After all, we come from different backgrounds. We all look at the world differently. Many of us have different experiences.

These differences, of course, add up. These differences have consequences across the board.

It is no surprise that people feel, somehow, some way, frustrated and less successful in their lives.

And most of the time, this is due to something that is very specific to them.

Two people may come from the same background, but they have made different decisions, and these choices have different implications. These implications trigger a chain reaction that leads to totally different paths and results.

Still, despite seeming differences, one common reason why people fail to live up to their potential is procrastination. In other words, they fail precisely for the same reason as my friend Bobby.

Therefore, one of the biggest obstacles in execution of activities towards your most important goals is procrastination.

It is All Your Choice

You have to understand that if you want your life to change for the better, you have to take action. You can't just wish a better reality for yourself.

It's not going to drop on your lap. You're not going to step into it. You're not going to stumble upon it.

As the old saying goes, the definition of insanity is doing the exact same thing over and over again, expecting a different result each time.

Regardless of whether that old saying was actually first said by no other than Albert Einstein, it doesn't matter. Its truth persists to this day: if you want a different result, you have to change what you're doing.

Here's the problem. Most people can't get to that point. They can't do what they need to do to change their life's direction.

What Makes Procrastination So Hard

Procrastination is a serious problem because of the fact that it's so obvious. Nothing is more frustrating than having the answer in front of you and being unable to implement the answer for whatever reason. That's what procrastination is.

When people procrastinate, it's not like they're clueless as to what they should be doing. They know full well the decisions they need to make. In fact, in many cases, it's very clearly laid out in front of them because they are walking a path that other successful people have walked in the past. This is not rocket science.

In fact, in the United States, for example, if you want to become a member of the middle class, and I'm talking about running a household that makes $60,000 a year, you only need to do two things. You need to be married, and both marriage partners have to have jobs that require a college degree. That's all you need to do.

In fact, in many major metropolitan areas, you don't have to have a college degree to become a member of the middle class. There are many well paid plumbers, roofers, and HVAC specialists. Many of these just require a vocational training certificate and a high school diploma. It's not rocket science.

But the problem is, most people struggle despite the fact that the roadmap in front of them is crystal clear.

The truth is, most people cannot get to that point. They can't do what they need to do to change their life's direction.

Despite the fact that they have all this information in front of them, despite the fact that they have seen people go through this path before to reach success and happiness, they can't do it.

This is the case even though they know what's really important and they know what's right for them.

Procrastination Goes Beyond Thinking

The problem with what I just described is that it all takes place in your head. You can get an intellectual realization or even an emotional revelation of what you need to be doing.

That's all great and everything, but the problem is, as long as it stays in your head, nothings going to happen.

It's actually quite frustrating because you can see the logic of the actions you need to take. It's crystal clear. But until and unless you take these clear intellectual realizations and turn them into action, your life is not going to change.

The reason for this is simple: the world doesn't care about your feelings. Seriously.

You may be all pumped up because you're thinking that you have this clear game plan in your head on how to succeed, how to go from Point A to Point B, and how to get things done.

Congratulations. You have managed something that most people are able to manage.

You may feel really strongly about it. You may feel that you're on the cusp of something great. You might even think that there's some sort of breakthrough in your life that's about to happen.

But until and unless you translate those feelings or sense of emotional urgency into action that other people can see, hear, touch, taste or smell, you're just fooling yourself.

You are just dragging out the inevitable. You are just delaying the creeping realization that you are wasting your life because you keep kicking the can down the road.

The world doesn't care about your feelings. All it cares about are results.

Once you translate what's going on in your head into actual action, that's when the world sits up and pays attention. That's when you change your personal world.

Because it's one thing to say that "I need to get a high school diploma" or "I need to finish the few units that I need to get a bachelor's degree in college." Anybody can say those things. But actually sitting down and doing them takes effort, focus, discipline, and energy. It definitely takes willpower.

When you're able to do that, you rise above the thousands, if not hundreds of thousands of other people who realize the same thing.

Please understand that whatever it is you are struggling with, maybe it's your weight, maybe it's your income, maybe it's the quality of your relationships, or maybe it's your self esteem, a lot of people are also struggling with the same issues. There's no shortage of people with those concerns. What separates those who succeed and who overcome is action.

Feelings are Not Enough

Everybody's got feelings. Everybody's got all sorts of intentions and motivations. A lot of these may be heartfelt. A lot of these may burn bright with passion. We may even reach the point where we smell the change coming.

That's awesome. But until and unless you actually change the way you behave, the world will not care. In fact, the world won't even notice. Seriously.

Everybody talks a good game. There's no shortage of that. But once you start making different decisions, and this is translated in your behavior, the world starts noticing. That's when it starts to judge you. That's when you either get rewarded or penalized.

It All Boils Down to Action

I hope it's abundantly clear to you that if you want to go anywhere in life, you have to take action. This is what makes procrastination so dangerous.

Please note that I did not say "worrisome," nor did I say "problematic." I said "dangerous." Why? Procrastination kills. That's the bottom line.

I know that you might be thinking that this is over dramatic. You may be thinking that I'm just blowing things out of proportion. But if you don't view every single day of your life as a gift, then procrastination is slow suicide. It is day-to-day self murder.

There's really no any other description that does justice to the harm that procrastination brings to the table.

Think about it, procrastination blocks you from taking the necessary action you need to take right here, right now, to get your life to the next level. You already know this. If you don't, you may want to sit down and put things together.

It doesn't take much effort to wrap your mind around the idea that each day that you get when you wake up in the morning is a day that you will never get back.

You can borrow money, you can go to the bank, you can pick up the phone and talk to a friend or a family member, and you can get money. That's not the problem.

But with time, you're out of luck. Once a minute passes, it's gone for good. This is why it's really important to understand how procrastination destroys your life by giving you the illusion that you have all the time in the world.

It's not unusual for a lot of people to get stuck in this holding pattern where they're thinking that they have all this mental realizations and emotional urgency, and it's only a matter of time until they get their act together.

Well, that's a lie that people keep telling themselves. Because the world is not going to change. The world and your situation is not going to change one bit until you take action.

It is no surprise that among people who continue to struggle, at some level or another, procrastination is part of the mix.

In many cases, it's not front and center. In many other situations, it is. But whatever the case may be, and whatever particular details may be different in your specific case, procrastination is still part of the picture.

Procrastination Doesn't Just Rob You of Success and Mental and Emotional Contentment

I wish I could tell you that procrastination, as dangerous as it is, only robs you of your ultimate potential as well as your personal contentment. In such a situation, it may even be forgivable to think that procrastination's damage can be limited in some way. But it isn't.

Believe it or not, procrastination's ill effects are not just mental and emotional. They also physically affect you. Indeed, procrastination decreases your life chances.

In a 1997 study released by the American Psychological society led by researchers Roy Beaumeister and Diane Tice out of Case Western Reserve University, procrastination leads to physical effects that degrade life's chances over the long haul. We're talking about illness, physical stress, and a consistent inferior performance.

The study had many different experiments. In one experiment, 60 students were told, at the beginning of their academic semester, the due date of their term paper. They were also informed that if they could not turn in the paper on time, they will get an automatic extension. The extension date was specific.

During this period, students were asked to fill out a report involving any visits to health care providers. They also had to fill out some questionnaires during the last week of their class. These questionnaires measure the level of procrastination exhibited by the students.

Please note that the students also had to fill out a questionnaire regarding their health during the first month of their class.

Comparing the two questionnaires, the researchers concluded that although procrastinating brought some short term health benefits due to lower levels of stress and better physical health, these were short-lived.

People who are not procrastinators were stressful at the beginning of the semester. They were looking forward to the deadlines and they reported more stress.

However, as time went by, the survey reports of procrastinators showed increasing levels of stress. The non procrastinators had lower levels of stress and illness.

The conclusion is, when you procrastinate, you make things harder on yourself physically, emotionally and mentally as you get closer and closer to the deadline.

The stress is cumulative and it impacts your life chances. This is not just happening in your head. It can translate to illness as this study showed.

The Bottom Line

If you want to become a more successful, effective, and happier person, you have to figure out how to stop procrastinating.

Seems pretty straightforward, right? It seems like you might even be tempted to think that there is some sort of one-size-fits-all, magic bullet solution to the problem of procrastination.

This is a problem. There is no such thing. Just because something works for your friend, it doesn't mean that it works for you.

Different people have different reasons for procrastinating. Different people react and respond to different "solutions" to procrastination.

If you were to apply some sort of cookie cutter solution that applies to all people at all times, in all situations, then it would be a beautiful world indeed. It definitely would be a simpler world. Unfortunately, such a situation doesn't exist.

This book teaches you how to craft a personal framework that will help you get out from under procrastination.

This framework is going to be filled in by you. You're going to have to pay attention to what's going on in your situation. You have to be mindful of your personal circumstances and tweak this framework so you can solve your procrastination problem once and for all.

Instead of ramming down some sort of magical solution down your throat, I'm going to teach you how to piece together a procrastination solution that makes sense in the context of your specific personal circumstances.

Again, there is no magical, one-size-fits-all solution. Be very suspicious of any productivity or self improvement guide that claims there is.

The best anybody can give people who are struggling with procrastination is a framework. That's precisely what you would get with this book.

Chapter 1: Understanding the Biggest Obstacle To Execution

To solve any problem, you must first start with a definition that works for you. It's very hard to solve any problem if you are unclear or fuzzy regarding the problem you're trying to solve in the first place.

This definitely applies to procrastination. We discussed in introduction how procrastination is the biggest obstacle in achieving your goals. Before working towards removing this obstacle, we need to clearly understand this.

But what makes this case tricky is that there is really no iron-clad definition that works for all people at all times. You just have to piece together a contextual or situational definition that fits your particular set of circumstances.

While there is a classic definition of procrastination, which involves putting things off in favor of other activities, for most people, that's neither here there. It seems too broad or it doesn't go far enough.

One way to come up with a clear working definition of procrastination is to first identify what it isn't.

What Procrastination Isn't

A lot of people confuse procrastination with laziness. These are actually two totally different things.

When you're lazy, you just don't want to do anything. You don't have the energy, motivation or even strength to do the task at hand. Regardless of what it is, you're just not going to do it. It's just not going to happen.

With procrastination, however, you may be motivated, pumped up and energized to do a lot of things. The problem is you're not motivated to do what you need to do. This is the big difference from laziness.

Procrastination is not a question of energy level. It has nothing to do with not knowing what to do or not operating out of some sort of emotional urgency. In fact, if you think about it, the fact that a lot of people are struggling with procrastination is specifically due to the fact that they are emotionally caught up in the situation.

They know what they should be doing, and it frustrates them that they'd rather do something else. They know what the negative consequences of kicking the can down the road are but, regardless, they just feel that they don't want to do what they should be doing. They may do an awesome job with other things.

For example, instead of working on your midterm paper, which accounts for 60% of your grade, you focus on cleaning your room. After that, you focus on cleaning your car. After that, you walk your girlfriend's dog and possibly help her clean up her apartment.

While all these other alternative activities are important in their own right, you know full well what you should be doing. You know full well what is more important as far as your choices of activities are right now because if you fail that class, you might have to repeat that class. It might get in the way of you getting into the right graduate school or getting into graduate school at all.

It has a lot of consequences and this is what eats you up. This has nothing to do with not having the ability to do it or not thinking that it's important enough. In fact, it's the precise opposite. You know that it's important. You know it has a lot of consequences and that's what's eating you up.

Please understand that when people struggle with procrastination, they do so on a deep personal level. In many cases, it's just driving them nuts. They know they should be doing certain things but, for the life of them, they can't seem to be able to do it.

Defining procrastination in terms of laziness is not doing you any big favors.

Procrastination, again, has nothing to do with low energy. It has nothing to do with confusion. It has nothing to do with not knowing what to do. In fact, you may have a clear idea of what you need to do, and you may be pumped up about the benefits you would get if you were able to do it. But still, you kick the can down the road.

A Clear Working Definition

The clearest and widest working definition of procrastination is that it involves doing something else other than what we should be doing. In other words, procrastination is all about misdirected energy and focus.

You have only a certain amount of willpower in any given day, but you focus those resources on things that may have a lower return or you know full well are not all that important. Maybe they're easier for you to do. Perhaps they're more pleasurable. Possibly, they seem more fun. Whatever the case may be, you devote your willpower to those things maybe with the intention of coming back to the stuff that actually matters most.

The problem is you only have so much willpower in a day. When you grapple or struggle with procrastination, you burn willpower at a very high rate. If you're like most people, you constantly find yourself with very little willpower left to devote to the things that matter most after you've done everything else.

Procrastination is also a coping mechanism to emotional triggers. When people get stressed about a task at hand, most people don't just dive in head long. They don't do that. Most people deal with the emotional stress by taking a side trip to other tasks that deliver payoffs but are not as important or as pressing as the task at hand.

Just like with the example that I gave earlier, there are emotional payoffs for cleaning up your room. Maybe there are certain things in your room that you have been meaning to throw out or clean up for a long time now. Well, when you were assigned that midterm, all of a sudden, you found the time to do things that you've been delaying all this time. Funny how that works, right?

This happens to people quite a bit. It turns out that when it comes to procrastination, people deal with a hierarchy of things that they would procrastinate on.

At the bottom are the ones that have the most impact on their lives yet are the most intimidating. For the life of them, they'd rather not do them. They'd look for anything and everything except those things.

So, what do they do? They go to the next option, which are things that while unpleasant and while unpleasant, are "easier" emotionally and mentally to process than the ones that they'd rather avoid.

I hope you see how this works out so. It's all comparative. If you did not have that midterm paper, chances are you probably wouldn't even bother cleaning up your room. You probably would go back to what you normally do and play video games, hang out with you girlfriend or just chill with your friends.

However, with the midterm hanging over your head, you'd be surprised as to how much energy and focus you have to do the things that you normally procrastinate about. This is a key feature of procrastination: It is comparative.

Don't think that there is some sort of set formula to procrastination where people just hold off on doing something and refuse to do anything else at all. That's laziness or absolute fear. That's not procrastination.

Finally, procrastination can become a mental habit. Why? We choose to respond to a set of stimuli this way over and over again. As long as we get a pretty standardized reward from this behavior, it starts to set in. Eventually, this becomes our default mental reaction to certain stimuli.

In other words, if we are presented with difficult tasks or tasks that scare us doesn't emotionally sit well with us, we start going through this automatic comparison, and we find the energy, motivation, and will part to do certain things we'd normally would procrastinate on.

Be clear on how you process tasks in your daily life. Identify how you procrastinate. Figure out its patterns so you can start solving this problem.

In the next chapter, I'm going to go into the reasons why people procrastinate. In Chapter 3, we're going to start going through effective strategies that enable people to finally beat procrastination.

Chapter 2: Why Do People Procrastinate and Fail To Take Action?

Like I said in the definition section of this book, different people have different reasons for procrastinating. Everybody's different. We all have different lives. We face different circumstances.

Still, if you look beyond these differences, a common pattern emerges. People procrastinate precisely because they're looking for the path of less resistance. Please note that I did not say least resistance. In other words, they're just comparing the different options in front of them and they go with something they think is easier to do, easier process and easier to make sense of.

It also doesn't take a genius to figure out that when somebody keeps going through this process to get the reward of feeling relief because they're not dealing with the stuff that they need to deal with, this easily becomes a mental habit.

You have to understand that all your habits at some level or other are chosen. Take the case of smoking. When somebody first starts to smoke cigarettes, they probably thought, "Smoking is cool." Maybe they saw an ad somewhere or they see people they like smoking, and they like what they see. So, they pick up a cigarette and light it and inhale.

The problem is cigarette smoke is very noxious. They cough. It hurts their lungs. In many cases, if they breathe in too quickly or too deeply, they get a nasty head rush. It's safe to say that for most smokers, their very first time is not actually a smooth and satisfying experience, but they chose to do that. When they choose to do it again, maybe they cough less.

Sooner or later, the rush that they get, thanks to the nicotine in their bloodstream, produces enough pleasure that outweighs the physical hassle they go through. They no longer stop thinking about how scratchy their throats feel and, instead, they look forward to the buzz.

While nicotine is a stimulant, a lot of people interpret its stimulating effect as calming or relaxing. This is all a mental illusion. Regardless, once people start desiring that biochemical effect, they have developed a habit.

Procrastination is no different. It is a course of action that delivers a steady reward. The reward is relief from having to deal with something that gives you so much stress and intimates you. It doesn't matter whether you did something that is less intimidating or something that's completely fun. What's important is you get that relief.

You don't have to deal with the midterm paper. You don't have to deal with the big decision of choosing whether to go to graduate school or get a job after college. You don't have to deal with the decision of working out a very important issue in your relationship because there is something more fun like sex available.

Do you see how this works? And it easily becomes a mental habit because you get such a heavy reward.

What are People Trying to Avoid Anyway?

People procrastinate out of fear due to the consequences of the main project because of certain benefits it brings. However, they also know that there are certain things that could go wrong if they mess up. It's a heavy responsibility.

A lot of times, people are just simply resistant to change They think that working on this project involves having to learn something new or grappling with something that they haven't seen before. It seems a bit too much. They'd rather stick to doing something that they are familiar with. Regardless, there's fear in the mix.

In other situations, people procrastinate because they feel that they'd brother not put in the effort to learn how to do something or to learn how to do it right.

Please understand that this is not a question of energy. Instead, it's a question of willingness to change. This is not about laziness. There are many people who are hard workers as long as it involves certain tasks that are predictable, well-known, and well-worn. In other words, they're not dealing with a set of new parameters. They're dealing with something that they know.

When people feel that they have to learn something new or they might be pushed out of their comfort zone, this gives them reason to pause and stop. This then becomes an issue of effort. However, at the end of the day, it's really about fear of change.

A lot of this fear also has something to do with people's estimation of their personal competence. If you're a person with low self-esteem, you're more likely to procrastinate because you feel that you're not all that capable. You feel that the new project that involves learning something new or a certain level of complexity might be just simply too much for you.

You have such a low view of your ability to adapt, to change, and to overcome that it becomes mentally and emotionally attractive to you to just look for something else to do other than that activity that would push you to level up.

See the differences? Regardless of these differences, they all lead to the same place.

What's at Stake?

Since procrastination can become habitual, just like with any habit, this can lead to changes in your brain structure. In a study out of Ruhr Universally Bochum published in 2018 in the journal Psychological Science, researchers studied two parts of the brain linked to people's tendency to procrastinate.

According to the study, the amygdala, which is a structure shaped like an almond on the temporal lobe side, and the DACC or dorsal anterior cingulate cortex are involved in a power play. The amygdala processes emotions and helps us control our motivations. The DACC, on the other hand, takes info from the amygdala and determines what the body would do.

The researchers worked with 264 subjects and they asked these individuals to fill out a survey regarding how proactive they are. According to survey results and brain scans, procrastinators usually have a larger amygdala.

There's also a weaker connection between this structure of the brain and the DACC. People who don't procrastinate have a normal-sized amygdala and a normal connection between the DACC and it.

The researchers suggest that this interplay between the DACC and amygdala can impact procrastination levels. If the relationship between these two structures of the brain are somehow impaired, people tend to procrastinate more.

According to one of the authors of the study, Erhan Genc, "Individuals with a larger amygdala may be more anxious about the negative consequences of an action - they tend to hesitate and put things off."

Generally speaking, this is not a problem but if there is a corresponding degradation of the connection between the DACC and the amygdala, people have a harder time dealing with their emotions and filtering out distractions. The result is procrastination.

The study suggests that just having a big amygdala, in of itself, doesn't automatically lead to procrastination. There has to be a corresponding weakness in the connection with the DACC for procrastination to happen.

Chapter 3: Change Your Mindset to Execute On Your Most Important Tasks

The first step to fixing your procrastination habit is to change your mindset. A lot of people procrastinate as a coping mechanism. It's their default solution to certain situations.

If you look at certain stimuli a different way, chances are you won't use procrastination as a solution. That's the bottom line. For example your default reaction to any kind of task that involves learning something new or making hard judgment calls is to kick the can down the road, you can turn things around by looking at things differently.

What if you're not afraid? What if your defaulter reaction is not to look at the project as something too complicated, too convoluted, and simply too difficult for you to handle? Without that negative emotional initial response, chances are procrastination wouldn't be your first option. You wouldn't give yourself that option.

Think of the last time you were presented with a project that you thought was interesting. Maybe it's a school assignment. Perhaps it's a book that you're supposed to read. Possibly, it's a social engagement. You were supposed to meet interesting people. Whatever it is, your initial attitude towards it or your starting mindset plays a big role in how you perceive a situation.

Don't think that just because you are given a task that the only way to respond to it is to be afraid. Get that idea out of your head. You have a lot more control over the situation than you think. A lot of it has to do with your assumptions and expectations about the project.

Unfortunately, a lot of people have fear as their default mindset. Other people operate out of a sense of obligation. Unfortunately, working from a sense of obligation can only go so far. It can easily become a chore. You can easily look at your situation as a hopelessly boring routine and mindless.

Other people look at tasks and they are reminded of how stuck they are.

It doesn't matter how easy the task is. You may have done it several times before. In fact, you may know it like the back of your hand, but it doesn't matter. The moment you become aware of the project this obligation that you need to fulfill, your mind feels stuck. You say to yourself, "Not this again. Why do I have to keep doing this? Isn't there's something better. Is this all that I'm capable of?"

Please understand that whether you are fearful, operating out of a sense of obligation, or feeling stuck and the reactions, these are all happening in your mind. I need you to come back to that central point because it may seem like your reaction is the only logical and reasonable reaction to the stimuli you're getting, but that's just you.

You must know that two different people who experience the same set of stimuli can easily you walk away with two completely different interpretations. How come? They have different mindsets. They expected different things. They assume different things and that's why do they responded to the same set of objectively the same set of stimuli in totally different ways.

For example, two people are standing on a street corner and a very expensive Mercedes Benz stops at the stoplight.

One guy looks at this sleek, very beautiful piece of German automotive engineering genius and says to himself, "There's no way in a million years I can afford a car like that. The rich get richer; the poor get poorer.

At that exact moment, the guy next to him looks at the exact same car and thinks to himself, "How can I afford a car like that? What must I do to be able to afford something as beautiful as that?"

Note the difference in their thought patterns. One person looked at the car and all he could see was his limitations. In fact, he ruled himself out from ever owning such a car because he said, "I cannot afford that."

That's a statement of fact. There is no gray area in that statement. That person is stating a statement of fact. There is no possibility of that person working, making arrangements, coming up with some sort of plan to come up with the money to buy that car. Instead, he just flat-out says that's just not going to happen.

The other person, on the other hand, doesn't say a statement. Instead, he asks a question. "How can I afford a car like that?" He follows that up with a more specific question, "What do I need to do to afford a car like that?"

These very different statements reflect very different mindsets. One person has resigned himself to a certain outcome. It's very easy to see what that outcome is. The other person, on the other hand, gave himself a challenge.

Whenever you come across the question "What must I do?" or "How do I do this?" or "How can I do this?" these are invitations for people to tap into the almost unlimited amount of imagination, resourcefulness, and creativity that all of us are capable of.

Please understand that just because we're capable of these doesn't mean that we are able to follow through. However, at the very least, by reacting with a question that begs action, the second guy positions himself to possibly owning a Mercedes Benz.

Welcome to the power of mindset. You can beat procrastination by changing your mindset.

Just because you have assigned a project that seems problematic to you because of a past experience doesn't mean that your current experience has to suck. Sure, you've seen it before. However, just because you have experienced problems in the past, it doesn't mean that you're going to have a problem now.

You can choose to do things differently. At the very least, you can choose to learn from your past experiences to make your current situation turn out better. You have a lot more choice over your situation than you give yourself credit for.

Be aware of your mindset. Maybe the reason you had such a tough time in the past was because you automatically felt it was impossible. Perhaps you thought that it was automatically too complicated, too convoluted and just takes too much time, effort, and energy, and it's not worth the bother.

Now is your chance to turn things around. Maybe now is the time for you to look at things that you normally run away from or avoid in a completely different light. In other words, when you change what you choose to assume about the task in front of you, you can make progress in resisting the urge to kick the can down the road.

Since procrastination can be a mental habit, you need to change your mental reward system.

Remember it's very easy to get triggered by your initial perception of a project. You may think that you've seen it before. You may think that there are certain things about the task you're supposed to do that they are too similar to problematic experiences in the past. In your mind, this is enough to just trigger your tendency to dodge that project.

In other words, you procrastinate because you're looking for that quickly reward of relief. You're not doing what you should be doing and it's perfectly okay because you feel that you're doing something else. At the back of your head, you know you're just avoiding.

Eventually, you will have to confront this project. The deadline will come. The consequences will be felt. It's only a matter of time.

Change your mental reward. The trigger is the same. However, change your mental reward. Instead of feeling relief because you have procrastinated, feel guilty. Allow yourself to feel lousy. Make procrastination burn.

Normally, it feels good. You think you've put one over. You think you've bought some time. You think you have handled the situation as best you could.

No, you didn't. You're just postponing the inevitable. Eventually the bill has to be paid. Ultimately, the deadline will come. It's only a matter of time.

Instead of feeling relief, feel stressed out. Feel a sense of anxiety. Feel let down. Feel guilty. Allow yourself to beat yourself up emotionally because you are not solving your problem.

Regardless of how you feel, make sure that it is not relief because that relief that you used to feel when you procrastinate is an illusion. You know it and people who depend on you know it.

Next, learn to rewire your habitual action. When you get triggered because a project or an obligation scares you, your habitual action, of course, is to procrastinate. Ask yourself, "Is there another way?"

If you're completely honest with yourself, you know there is. One way, of course, is to just jump in with both feet and forget about your fears or your emotional state, and just slam into the project.

Is it going to be pleasant? Usually, it isn't. Is it going to be easy? Of course not.

However, the more you do this as a habitual response, the more you would be able to figure things out and, most importantly, the more you will get used to it.

Instead of automatically heading for the exits or hitting the snooze button or postponing because you're postponing, you plow straight ahead.

Alternatively, you can break down what's in front of you and you hit it in bits and pieces. Allow yourself to feel satisfied if you have successfully handled a smaller portion. That's okay. It may be a baby step, but it's still a step forward. That's right. It's a step in the right direction.

Learn to rewire your habitual action and response to the same cues. You know that you want the same rewards. You want the sense of relief or the sense of accomplishment so you change your behavior.

If you change your reward to a sense of anxiety because you procrastinated, that works as well. However, that's a negative reward.

If you want to rewire your habitual reaction, you have to pair it with a positive reward. In this case, the only way you will give yourself permission to feel relief is if you have actually done the work. It doesn't have to be complete, but at least reward yourself for doing the work.

Finally, change your assumptions about your projects. Think of a time when you took on a project, a task, an assignment, or a social engagement, and something great happened.

Let me tell you, even if you think that you are the worst person in the world or the biggest loser that you know, you probably have done things right at least once in your life. Think about that incident.

It turns out that regardless of how fearful or anxious you were coming in, things worked out. Things weren't as bad as you thought they would be. Always come back to that. Use that as an opening in you changing your assumptions and expectations about the scary project or assignment or task in front of you.

Tell yourself, "This is going to be one of those. This is going to be exactly like that situation.

Instead of fearing, I should get excited because I might discover something. I might learn something new. I might be able to do things better."

Believe it or not, changing your mindset regarding the task in front of you actually changes the outcome you get.

In a 1999 study out of UCLA, college freshmen were asked to imagine doing better on a test. Another group was asked to think about the final grade that they would get from an exam.

According to a study published in 1999 in the Personality and Social Psychology Bulletin, the first group did much better on the actual exam than those who imagined what their ultimate grade would be.

How come? Well, a few days before the midterm exam, study participants either mentally thought about the process of performing well in the exam or they simply imagined getting a good grade.

Those who imagined the process did better. The reason, of course, is because of their emotional state. Since they imagined an optimal process, they were able to short-circuit students' normal emotional reactions.

It's easy to get tripped up. It's easy to let your worst fears become self-fulfilling prophecies. By thinking about the process instead of the ultimate grade, you allow yourself to relax about the project. It's not as scary as you initially thought.

Some Warnings

Don't think that you just need to sit down and think about your assumptions and expectations, shift them to something more positive or more affirming, and you will be okay. I wish it were that easy.

Instead, you have to be careful. Don't let your mindset changes remain at the mental level. At this point, it's just all intellectual. You're just moving mental furniture around.

Mindset changes can only lead to the right actions if they have an emotional component. That's right. Get pumped up. Feel optimistic. Feel the possibility.

This is the opposite of feeling stuck. This is the opposite of feeling like you're a deer caught in headlights and you have this car coming at you.

How do you trigger this emotional component?

You can change up your work schedule. You can change the order in which you do things. You can reprioritize the perceived value of the things that you to do in any given day. Whatever it is that you need to do, do it to change your sense of emotional urgency.

Other Changes You Might Want to Try

One approach is to just change your ritual. Maybe you typically do certain things before a "scary" task. You might want to change those things this time around. Maybe by doing so, you're less likely to procrastinate.

Another approach is to think about when was the last time you were able to tackle a problem regardless of how seemingly scary it was and do an amazing job? Can you identify where you were? Why not go to that same place and do the same action?

Another technique is to give yourself a few minutes to feel gratitude. You can also think of the last time you felt pride or contentment and focus on the emotional state there.

When you any of these, you short-circuit the normal emotional reaction you get to "difficult" projects. You're more at ease. You're more likely to look at things from a different perspective. You're more likely to look at things from a fresh set of eyes, and this could lead to a change in your mindset that can lead to you behaving differently about the task.

The good news is regardless of what you do, if you see some improvement, you can choose to be inspired by it. You can see that this is doable. It may have been impossible in the past. Previously, it may have automatically triggered you to procrastinate, but not this time.

Feel free to mix and match the techniques described above. What's important is that you tried them all out and tried to tweak them so they work optimally in your specific situation.

Chapter 4: Turn to Technology when Self-Control Fails

I understand that you know what you should be doing. You know what your problems are and judging by the fact that you're reading this book, you already know the solutions. At the very least, you have a fairly good idea of how to get your problem under control.

The issue is not identifying the problem and being clear on the answers. Instead, the issue is going through with the solution. There are many things in life that are easier said than done and overcoming procrastination through increased levels of self-control is one of them.

Please understand that your self-control will fail that's why you are reading this book. That's the reason you're having a tough time with procrastination.

You can turn to technology to try to contain or reduce your procrastination habit. You can use apps that reduce distractions. They force you to work on the task that you have assigned yourself and nothing else. They can also help you manage your time and redirect your mind so you are less likely to procrastinate.

Of course, these apps are not bulletproof. The good news is the more you do them, the higher the chance you will get the results that you're looking for.

To some people, this is app-based solution is a non-starter. To others, it works like a charm. Most people are somewhere in the middle. Still, it doesn't hurt to use a variety of apps and software that can reduce procrastination.

In fact, in a 2015 study published by the Cornell Higher Education Research Institute, 675 students participated in a program was held in Stanford University. All the students downloaded software that tracked their online activities. The students were split up into three groups and then there's another group of students, which is the control group.

For Group 1, students gave themselves a time allotment every day that allowed them to view distracting content using their mobile devices. This content ranged from Facebook, ESPN, and BuzzFeed. After the allotted time is over, the software in their mobile device would block them from accessing these sites.

During the nine-week study period, the students assigned themselves to an average 2.7 hours every day to viewing distracting materials. On average, during the whole nine weeks, students went over their limit four times. This happened even though the software gave them an early-morning email reminder of their content-viewing limit.

In another group, students received a notification from their app every half hour they spend on viewing distracting content. For this group, the software sent forty-eight reminders on average for each student.

In the final group, students were allowed to completely block off access to distracting websites in fixed time increments. They can do it for an hour, thirty minutes or fifteen minutes. This block takes place when they access course materials. In this group, very few students used this option. Only 1.7 times on average during the whole nine-week course the average blockage is thirty-eight minutes.

It turned out that among the three groups, those who committed to set their own time blocks and were forced to abide by that time block turned out to be more productive over the whole nine-week course. They also got higher grades on average than the other two groups, which didn't set limits on themselves.

This study highlights the fact that technology can work depending on the model. The studied app actually helped students commit to firm time limits.

The other takeaway is that just because you're using an app doesn't mean that you will get the results that you are looking for. You have to use an app that works best with the right method for self-control. In this case, it was commitment to a specific time window.

Chapter 5: Simplify Your Way to Action

A lot of people are scared stiff of taking action because they think that the project or assignment ahead of them is simply too frightening. What's so scary about it? Either they assume that it's too big or too complicated. They think about the project and they just freeze.

By simply breaking down your task into smaller, easier-to-do pieces, you can get rid of the fear factor. A project that used to seem so intimidating could actually look quite doable when you break it down into its smaller parts.

The Secret to Simplification

A lot of people think that as long as they break down a task into equal parts that they are necessarily simplifying the task. That's not the way to do it. To properly simplify a task, you have to break it down to the extent that each small piece or sub-task or action item doesn't take much physical and/or mental action. That's how you know you're on the right track.

Think of these as "micro-tasks." You know that you have broken it down easily when you can do a micro-task in less than fifteen minutes. You know you're doing it right if you are able to get it down to that size. Of course, the smaller, the better.

The next secret is to impose a strict time limit on yourself to handle each micro-task. In other words, don't give yourself all day to handle micro-tasks because if you did, you just defeated the purpose of this exercise. You actually added more work to your plate because what would have usually taken you a short period of time now takes forever when all the pieces are added together.

Don't do that. Instead, look at each micro-task and time yourself. See how you can improve your speed without sacrificing quality of your output. In fact, once you have sped up quite a bit, look to see if you can take some of the time that you save to improve the quality of your output. By sticking to a strict timeframe for each micro-task, you can boost your output and work quality.

How Do You Know When to Speed Up?

Once you go through a micro-task and it seems really easy, that's when you know you can speed up. This means you can take on one micro-task after another without feeling mentally or physically tired. The bottom line is once it becomes very comfortable for you, that is your cue to scale up.

A Pennsylvania States University study tried to uncover the psychology behind people's desire to complete tasks quickly.

In a series of experiments, University students were given the option of picking up a bucket at either two points of an alley. They were supposed to pick up a bucket and walk it all the way to the end of the alley. One bucket is closer to the end point while the other is nearer the starting point.

Interestingly enough, more study participants picked the bucket closer to the starting point. In other words, they had to walk a longer way to complete the task.

When study participants who chose this option were asked to explain their choice, they said they just wanted to get the whole thing over as quickly as possible. Picking the starting point bucket doesn't complete their task faster. In fact, it's the harder option.

Researchers were stumped as to why this is the case. They suspect it has to do with a psychological tendency to want to complete tasks as quickly as possible just for the sake of getting them done and over with sooner rather than later.

I suspect that this is the same operation regarding micro-tasks. People who are successful with micro-tasks want to get them over as quickly as possible and this leads to a sense of momentum.

Chapter 6: Crave Your Personal State of Flow

Believe it or not everybody enters a state of peak productivity. You might think you are the laziest or most procrastination-prone person on the planet but guess what? You have your own state of flow.

This is the point when you are able to just do challenging work very quickly and very smoothly. Instead of getting scared or feeling that you've just gotten sucked into a very problematic project, things just start to come to you and it feels so easy.

Please understand that this is otherwise challenging work. On a normal day, you'd have to put in a lot of energy and burn up a tremendous amount of willpower to get through these tasks. This is not a cake walk.

Still, when you are within your personal state of flow, if it seems that thing you just come to you. You're able to see the big picture. You're able to tap into your personal reservoir of imagination, creativity, and resourcefulness.

However you want to describe it, everything seems to fall into place and you are able to produce some of your best work. Believe it or not, even the worst procrastinators in the world have their state of flow. They have experienced something close to this at some point in the past.

The truth is everybody has the capacity to achieve a state of flow. You just either need the right internal or external stimuli to bring it on. In many cases, it's a combination of both.

What does this have to do with procrastination? The good news is simple: Procrastination melts in the face of "flow." The second piece of good news is you can achieve this personal state of flow on command. That's right. You can turn it into a habit. It doesn't have to be something that just happens to you when things just happened to line up. It doesn't have to be random chance.

This idea of flow was pioneered by the researcher Mihaly Csikszentmihalyi. What makes this tricky is that this is a subjective state of mind. You are caught in a deep level of engagement. Things just work when you are in a state of flow.

As you can imagine, this "state" has to be objective because different people respond to stimuli in different ways. Some people can achieve their state pretty much anywhere at any time. Other people have to have the right internal and external triggers for them to enter this state.

What really stood out in Csikszentmihalyi's research is that people in a state of flow are dealing with very challenging work yet they register a very high level of engagement and enjoyment. In other words, when you are being challenged to level up your skills and you're not emotionally intimidated, flow happens. You tend to produce your best work in these subjective states.

To determine the interplay between the external and internal factors on "flow" experience triggers, researchers at South Korea's Halla University surveyed 262 college students. They correlated self-reported performance, levels of procrastination, and motivation.

It turned out that students who were motivated internally tend to suffer from less procrastination. They are more likely to enter a state of flow. In other words, if you are motivated from within instead of your circumstances, you are more likely to achieve a state of flow and less likely to suffer from procrastination.

If you think about it, this makes all the sense in the world. If you rely on extrinsic or external triggers for your personal state of flow, chances are you are going to be waiting for a long time.

Please understand that some people are just configured for external stimuli. As much as they want, they can't trigger themselves with internal motivations. They have to find themselves in the right place at the right time surrounded by the right people for them to enter their state of flow.

The good news is if you work on triggering yourself through internal motivations to achieve a state of flow, you are less likely to procrastinate. This is good news because you have a higher degree of control over yourself. Compare this with trying to control your surroundings, other people, or the circumstances you find yourself in.

Talk about a tall order. Think about it. It's hard enough to change yourself. Can you imagine trying to change other people or control the people? Most of the time, that's just not going to happen. Most of the time, that's not an option.

I understand that this is a very difficult option for a lot of people because a lot of people are just extrinsically oriented, but if you want to trigger your personal high-productivity and high-creativity state of flow on command, you have to start with intrinsic or internal motivators.

Chapter 7: Hold Yourself Accountable

To beat procrastination, you can't just look at it as some sort of idealistic or academic exercise. You can't just look at this as your personal hobby project.

The problem with that type of thinking is that you're not really feeling the pain when you let yourself down. There's really not much on the line. Your efforts at trying to beat procrastination on a systematic basis can easily be dismissed as just one of the things that "you would like to do."

This is going to be a problem. Chances are, if you're like most people, you have a bucket list. These are the things that you would like to do or would like to experience right before you kick the bucket.

Unfortunately, we all know that the majority of people are only able to tick off a small tiny fraction of all the activities and experiences that they've put on their bucket list. That' just the way it is.

Unfortunately, if you're going to look at your efforts at beating procrastination as another bucket list item, you're probably not going to make it.

You have to hold yourself to account. This can't be just an intellectual exercise. This can't be just a to-do item or something that "would be nice" to achieve.

No. There has to be pain involved. There has to be some sense of loss or disappointment.

You Need to Make It Hurt

One way of holding yourself to account is to allow yourself to feel lousy if you procrastinate. You know when you drop the ball. You don't need people to remind you. You already know what it's like to procrastinate. You know what's at stake.

There's no need for somebody to step up to you and tell you that you're screwing up. You have to do it for yourself. You have to give yourself permission to feel bad when you procrastinate. The stakes are high.

In fact, you should take it to the next level. Don't just feel bad. Don't just feel inconvenienced.

Don't think that this is just another bump in the road. You have to level it up. You have to actually give yourself personal permission to emotionally beat yourself up.

I know you are not supposed to engage in negative internal monologues. It's usually a bad idea to say "I'm a loser" or "I can't make it," "I suck." However, in this situation, you have to give yourself an internal statement that sums up your disappointment with yourself.

I suggest that you phrase it in such a way that it doesn't kill your motivation down the road. It's also a good idea to avoid statements that program your mind to lackluster or sub-par performance.

Don't call yourself loser. Don't call yourself hopeless. But you have to come up with a statement that hurts enough for you to feel that you're holding yourself to account.

Otherwise, you really don't have any skill in the game. Basically, you're just looking at this whole project with "best efforts" mindset. We know how that plays out. Usually, it doesn't end well.

The Power of Forgiveness

The key is to feel the disincentive then quickly forgive yourself and move on.

In a 2010 study out of Carleton University in Canada published in the journal Personality and Individual Differences, 119 students were given assessments on procrastination levels. They also were tested on their ability and willingness to forgive themselves.

After they have taken the surveys, they then took midterm exams for their introductory psychology class. It turns out that the students who've forgiven themselves for procrastinating early on suffered less negative effects than those who did not forgive themselves. The other group was more likely to procrastinate. They tended to suffer worse grades.

The key takeaway here is that self-forgiveness is crucial to beating procrastination. It's important to note that the tendency to forgive oneself is not tied to whether the person got a good grade or not in the first midterm test. What's important is the person is willing to forgive himself or herself for procrastinating.

According to the researchers, forgiveness allows the individual to move past maladaptive behavior and focus on the upcoming examination without the burden of past acts to hinder studying. By feeling disappointed and allowing yourself to feel disappointed as a disincentive and then forgiving yourself, you can position yourself for better performance later on.

Adopt an Accountability Buddy System

Just like alcoholics, procrastinators can benefit tremendously from having a buddy or accountability partner monitor them as they try to beat procrastination. The key here it is to pick somebody you can trust.

It's also a good idea to document your efforts. Don't just rely on your buddy to give you a call or send you an email. You also have to monitor yourself. The way this works is that you tie your general entries to specific productivity targets on a day-to-day basis.

Don't just rely that your partner will automatically know what your productivity targets are. They wouldn't know. They're not mind readers. That's you responsibility to yourself.

You have to clue them in on what your targets are but, ultimately, you have to hold yourself responsible.

Indeed, in a study out of the Dominican University of California, people who put their goals down in writing and then share it with people who supported their goals were actually more likely to achieve their goals compared to people who just simply thought about having goals and never shared it with anybody and much less write it.

In a study involving 267 participants ranging from all walks of life, Dominican Psychology professor, Dr. Gail Matthews, randomly assigned different people to different groups.

The first group involved people who had unwritten goals. The second group was for people with written goals. Group 3 was for people with written goals and who committed to certain actions. Group 4 are people who wrote their goals, committed to a certain action and shared it with a friend and, finally, Group 5 is for people with written goals, commitments to actions and who also commit to giving progress reports to friends.

In Group 1, people were just asked to remember their goal or think about their goal.

In Group 2, the people were then asked to rate their goals in terms of difficulty, importance to them, the extent where they had the resources and skills to achieve their goals, their level of motivation and commitment for goal achievement and whether they have pursued this goal before. Finally, they were also asked if they had been successful in pursuing a similar goal.

At the conclusion of the study, people who were not asked to write down their goals showed the lowest level of achievement. Only 43% of them accomplished their goals or reported up to 50% completion rate.

The highest achieving group was Group 5. These are people who not only wrote their goals and committed to certain actions but were asked to give progress reports to somebody. This group reported 76% completion rate.

The bottom line is a bit of accountability goes a long way. The higher the amount of accountability, the higher the chance you won't procrastinate and actually follow through with your goals.

Chapter 8: Don't Hesitate to Scale Things Up Once Things Get "Easy"

The problem with procrastination is that once you think you've beaten it, it starts to come back. If you're not careful, it comes roaring back. In fact, I've seen it many times before, people who achieve some sort of progress beating back procrastination end up procrastinating much worse after enough time has passed.

If you don't want this to happen to you, you have to know how to scale things up because once things get easy, that's when you need to be on your guard because it's so easy to just let things slide. You may be thinking, "Well, I've beaten procrastination before so I can get away with slacking off everyone now and then." Don't be surprised when your cheat days start turning into cheat weeks and, before you know it, you're back to where you started.

The key here is to continuously challenge your ability to beat procrastination. Think of it as like a muscle. When you first start going to the gym, chances are you felt like hell after lifting weights.

However, if you have the discipline to work through the pain, things become easier for you. Your muscles adjust to the stress that you put on it, and they become leaner, bigger and stronger.

The same applies to your ability to beat procrastination. You have to continuously challenge that ability. Otherwise, it starts getting soft and you end up where you began.

How do you scale up? Focus on when things get easy. That's your cue to stepping things up.

One way to effectively step things up is to avoid the tendency to start new tasks until you have completely taken care of previous tasks. This truly overcomes procrastination and enables you to use the "easy" parts of your task to springboard or to push forward to harder parts of your task.

The key is to row with the momentum. Don't stop. It's a trap. Once you give yourself the luxury of stopping because things got easy, it's only a matter of time until you start backsliding.

Chapter 9: Finish What You Start

When people manage to start something, they are more inclined to finish it. The problem is procrastinators look at how big the project is, and they allow themselves to get intimidated at some level or other. Starting is not a problem. Most procrastinators can start, but good luck trying to get them to go all the way through.

It's kind of like climbing a huge mountain. Most procrastinators can get to the trail at the foothills of the mountain. That's not the problem. The issue is they look at the summit of the mountain and they think that this is just going to be murder so they start looking for something else to do.

The starting point is not the issue. Part of this is due to fact that a lot of people don't tap the power of starting. A lot of procrastinators assume that they have started and, for the most part, a lot of them can start but, at the end of the day, it's really all about not having the right mindset when they start. It's as if it's just an afterthought. They just go through the motions and then, all of a sudden, they freeze.

Repeat this enough times and people find themselves unable to start. They may give themselves all sort of reasons not to start.

The worst procrastinators didn't start out that way. At first, they were able to start but they got freaked out by their experiences. They found it harder and harder to start. The worst procrastinators are unable to start.

Just Start

One way to beat procrastination is to just start. Think of it almost as a mindless step forward. It doesn't matter where. It doesn't matter when. Just do it. Just start. It doesn't have to be perfect.

Once you start, keep pushing through. This enables you to get closer and closer to the end. It doesn't have to be perfect. It doesn't have to look good. Just do it. Eventually, you will find your rhythm and you will be able to hit your quality targets. Again don't let the perfect the enemy of the good.

Compare this with being unwilling to start at all. This is called the Zeigarnik effect named after the Russian psychologist, Bluma Zeigarnik. This effect describes the psychological phenomenon where people tend to remember unfinished tasks more than completed ones.

Zeigarnik came up with this idea based on his observation of waiters at a café. It seemed that the waiters who had incomplete tabs tended to remember those tabs more efficiently compared to when those tabs are paid for.

This suggests that when people have unfinished tasks, they tend to focus on those more in their minds. This is a serious problem for procrastinators because if you don't start, you tend to focus on the unfinished task or the task that you have yet to start. All this mental baggage starts to weigh you down. You start to worry about things that haven't taken place yet. You haven't even started.

The key is to start and keep pushing forward so you can complete.

Chapter 10: Embrace "the Art of Delaying"

Did you know that "active procrastination" can help some people feel motivate enough to power through tasks that they normally scared of? "Active procrastination" refers to delaying starting on a task so you can focus on more important tasks.

This strategy doesn't work across the board. Not all people respond favorably to this technique. Still, if you are a person who thrives under pressure and can handle a tremendous amount of stress, this might be the breakthrough you're looking for.

If you're like most people, however, who tend to slow down under stress, this might not be the way forward. Still, I'm throwing this out there so, regardless of your productivity orientation, you would at least have some options.

This idea of active procrastination was studied by researchers at McGill and Columbia University. They wanted to determine if there was such a thing as a "positive procrastinator." They published their results in the June 2005 issue of the journal Social Psychology.

In their study of 230 college students, they found that there is a subset of study participants who, on the surface, engaged in procrastination. However, when they looked at the personal effectiveness of these people, they actually are able to do more than classic procrastinators.

The latter group, of course, are the ones who are just paralyzed by intimidating tasks. They just cannot make any progress on tasks that seem too big or seem too complicated for them.

Digging deeper, researchers found that active procrastinators are more purposeful in their time management and their usage of time. They also tend to be more effective people. They use procrastination to generally challenge themselves while handle more urgent tasks. As you can well imagine, relatively few people fall under this grouping.

Chapter 11: Bundle Your "Must Do's with Your "Should Do's" and "Want to Do's"

Generally speaking, people have three types of tasks.

There are things that they need to do. These are our "must do's."

We have things that are important and can be very beneficial for us, but are not pressing. These are our "should do's."

Finally, there are things that we are curious about or are a lot of fun to us but are not particularly important and high priority. These are our "want to do's."

In an ideal world, if you are like most people, you would probably fill your daily schedule with the things that you'd want to do. These are the two things that you like .These are activities that are pleasurable and they don't feel like work.

Unfortunately, most of us have to focus on our "must do's." These are the activities that put food on the table.

Sadly, if we were just to focus on those, we probably won't get far in our careers and our businesses. We won't feel as fulfilled and content. This is where our "should do's" come in. They challenge us and they push our limits. They force us to innovate.

One effective way to beat procrastination is to establish a nice mix of these three types of tasks. Use your "want to do" list as a carrot. Most of the time, people procrastinate with the things that they should do.

Schedule your daily tasks in such a way that you alternate between the things that you want to do and the things you must do and should do. This takes some doing. There's no magical formula for this. You have to play it by ear.

However, after enough experimentation, you should be able to identify the ideal mix for yourself. If you set this up right, things that you otherwise struggle with or find unappealing or difficult (I am, of course, talking about your "should do" list) becomes manageable. You end up doing more of the things that push your life forward. Normally, these tasks are a burden to you. You'd rather not do them.

This technique was pioneered by Wharton Business School professor Catherine Milkman. She was inspired to come up with this concept and test it because when faced with going to the gym, she'd rather read a book.

According to the study she conducted, which was released in 2013 published in the journal, Management Science, study participants were more likely to cross off items on their "should do" list if these items were alternated or bundled with things that they'd like to do or want to do.

The experiment involved three groups of people that were given different incentives.

The first was the control group, which was given $25 Barnes & Noble gift cards for exercising thirty minutes.

The other group was loaned an iPod with audio novels of the participant's choice. They were to listen to these materials while doing the thirty-minute exercise.

The third group was loaned the iPod and given access to very addictive audio books. The big difference between this group and the previous group was that they could only use the iPod if they were at the gym doing exercises.

The three groups were observed over a ten-week period. It turned out that making sure that the iPod can only be accessed at the gym itself increased gym visits by the third group by 51% compared to the control group. This experiment proves that when we mix the things that we want to do with the things that we should do, we tend to procrastinate less and tackle more difficult tasks.

Chapter 12: Think Why You shouldn't Procrastinate and Rather Focus on Execution

Believe it or not, simply thinking about what could go wrong if you procrastinate or its negative long-term effects can actually motivate you to tackle the task that you have been putting off. Of course, this is not fool-proof. It all depends on how much effort and time you put into this.

You can't just sit down, look at your task and just quickly think about missing a deadline and, as a result, not getting that raise or promotion. For most people, that's not enough. You actually have to dwell on the disadvantages of procrastination.

One way to do this is to look at the task that you're struggling with and ask yourself, "Why should I do it?" A lot of people struggle with procrastination not because they don't know how to do things. It's not a question of technical proficiency or having access to the right information.

Instead, they lack motivation because they don't see a purpose or they're unclear about why they should do the task. Answering this question is a little trickier than you think. You shouldn't just look at personal benefits because if that's the case, it's very easy to see why you should do the task that you are assigned at work or school, for example. It's easy to see the negative effect it would have on your career and income. In the academic setting, it's very easy to see the negative effect on your grades.

That's not the issue. You have to look at this problem from a personal perspective. On a personal level, why would you want to do this? Does it challenge your imagination? Does it push you to be a more resourceful and creative person? Does it enable you to stretch outward the boundaries of your comfort zone? You have to think in these terms so you can get motivated enough regarding the benefits.

The next step is to ask yourself why you're procrastinating. At this stage, you're looking at the task from the other side. Ask yourself what's holding you back. Is there something that you fear about the project? Does it seem more complicated than it is? Does it appear that it's going to take a lot of your mental and emotional resources?

Once you have a nice list of the reasons you give yourself why you're holding back, the next step is to look at reality. Confront those reasons that you give yourself. Do they make any sense in light of reality?

It also helps tremendously if you've done something similar to the task before because if you did, it's obvious that it's not as hard as you think. It's not as impossible ask you think.

Believe it or not, when it comes to procrastination, a little self-awareness can go a long way. Figuring out why you procrastinate involves circumstantial and situational awareness. In other words, different circumstances might make you more vulnerable to procrastination.

Have you ever noticed that in certain settings or when certain things line up, you rarely procrastinate? It's as if you just sit down, you look at the task in front of you and you work on it until you knock it out? However, in other circumstances, you can find a thousand and one reasons why you should put things off.

Figure out why you do that when you find yourself in certain circumstances. This is all situational. Don't think that you're coming up with some sort of one-size, fits-all solution that works once and for all. It doesn't. There's no such thing. You have to always tie it into the greater context you find yourself in.

For a lot of people, simply figuring out why they procrastinate and when goes a long way in protecting them from falling into unproductive patterns. I'm not saying that this insight will solve your problem overnight but it does provide a tremendous amount of context and it makes it easier for you to get out from under your procrastination habit.

In the article "Mind Games Procrastinators Play," psychologists Lenora Nguyen and Jane Burka report that among the students that they studied, a bit of understanding regarding the roots of their procrastination habits were enough to weaken those habits. Just by being clear about the real reasons you procrastinate makes it easier for you do to eventually stop. This article was published in the journal from Princeton University.

Chapter 13: Reward Yourself after You Finish a Big Task

Another great way to help you overcome procrastination is to reward yourself after you take care of a big task. When you set a reward at the end of the process, you give yourself a tremendous incentive to start and keep going.

This is a bit tricky. It makes a lot of sense to reward yourself only after you have finished the project. This is how most incentive programs work. Companies will only pay for results. Most of the time, they don't pay you for "trying." In most situations, trying is simply not good enough.

You can try setting up an incentive reward for completion, but it's probably not going to be as effective if you reward yourself for the efforts you took. I suggest that you combine both. Reward yourself primarily for your effort but give yourself a lot more extra when you actually complete the task.

If you do this enough times, you start associating work or tasks that you normally find unappealing and intimidating with something more pleasurable. The more you reward yourself, the stronger the association becomes and this enables you to start on time.

I can't even begin to tell you how big of a deal this is. If you are a chronic procrastinator, you know that this is a big thing. In fact, if you are assigned a task that you are normally scared of or you think is a complete waste of time or is a hassle, your default reaction would be negative. You'd think of a million and one reasons not to start.

However, when combining rewarding yourself for your effort and completing the task, you break that mental association. You at least would want to give it a shot and start on time.

The good news is, oftentimes, this is all you need because once you get started and you keep at it, momentum builds. You start to realize that this is not as bad as you thought. This time around, things are falling into place.

The initial hesitation that you had and the fear were totally uncalled for and unjustified because this is actually cakewalk. Does that ever happen to you? Well, it happens to a lot of people. Their actual experience going through a task doesn't match their initial fear of it.

In 1992, University of Houston professor Robert Eisenberger published an article in the journal Psychological Review. It highlighted a phenomenon called "learned industriousness." He suggested that when people get rewarded for putting in high effort, this makes it easier for people to put in high effort in the future.

This flew in the face of how rewards are normally given. As I mentioned earlier, most companies don't reward you for trying. Professor Eisenberger found out that companies can benefit quite a bit for rewarding people for their effort instead of basing rewards solely on results.

This is due to the fact that people would like to be rewarded as they make progress towards the ultimate goal. Because if you were just going to reward people based on the result, most people would still find going through the process to produce those results intimidating. Their perception of the project hasn't really changed.

However, if you base a large part of the incentive in the actual process itself, you change people's minds. They are more eager to start. They are more likely to go through the process.

I've learned that Professor Eisenberger's concept of learn industriousness works best when you create internal milestones for yourself. Take a task that you're normally scared off. Break it down into milestones that culminate, of course, in its final completion. Reward yourself as you reach each milestone.

In the beginning, you probably would struggle to get the first two milestones out of the way. Starting takes a lot out of you. However, as you get used to the incentive system, knocking out the first two milestones become easier and easier, and you get further and further in the process. Eventually, you reach a point that you're able to go through that complete process repeatedly in a short period. This way, your mind isn't just focus on the nice reward at the complete end of the process. It may seem too far away.

By breaking down the project into smaller milestones and rewarding yourself as you reach them, you position yourself to not only start on time every time but to put maximum effort to reach as many milestones as possible. If you keep getting the same tasks at work or at your business, don't be surprised if you are able to handle what normally would be a difficult, challenging or intimidating task very easily and quickly.

Chapter 14: Visualize Yourself Free from Procrastination

Think of yourself as somebody who's completely free of procrastination. What would you look like? Imagine yourself in a typical work setting. What would you be doing? How would you be handling things differently?

This might seem a bit nebulous. A lot of people might struggle with this because it seems so open-ended. However, focus on an alternative self being able to make hard decisions and put in hard work.

Once you're able to do that, pick a specific time in your future with a specific set of circumstances.

For instance, you're a college student and you are dealing with a lot of midterm essays and you have to study for a final exam for many difficult courses. Imagine yourself at finals time or at midterms time performing at peak levels.

Then try to trace that performance to you graduating with honors, maybe a magna cum laude or even a summa cum laude. Tie that into getting a high-paying, prestigious, high-impact job at a fast-rising company or at a large, well-known company.

Imagine yourself being free of procrastination in that high-powered setting and zooming like a rocket up the corporate ladder. A lot of people get pumped up when they visualize certain alternative realities.

You have to understand that when you visualize, you're not just flashing mental images in your imagination. These are rarely emotionally neutral. You feel pumped up, motivated, inspired.

Once you detect these emotions, you have all you need to start and keep going. In other words, you can combat procrastination with the emotional states you get through visualization.

You don't have to get married to the images that come to mind. You don't have to say to yourself, "Well, I have to achieve those things because they're my ultimate goals." That's not the point. The point is to get emotionally pumped so you can blast through the current task that seems to be holding you back.

This future self that you're connecting to can give you the emotional firepower you need to overcome procrastination in the here and now. Your future may well turn out to be quite different from what you imagine to be. That's okay. What's important is you have a clear enough picture of your future self who is free from procrastination.

This is not just a simple mind game. This has actually been proven to work. In a 2015 study published in the Carleton University Research Virtual Environment, 193 college students were split up randomly into two groups. One group was assigned focused meditation; the other group was assigned to focus on their future self.

In the course of four weeks, participants were asked to listen to audio recording twice a week. Over the four-week period, participants had to fill out a starting point questionnaire, halfway questionnaire, and completion questionnaire. The questionnaires measured two things: how the people are connected to their future self in terms of vividness of imagery and empathy. It also tested their procrastination levels.

The study showed that when people focused on their future self-image and created an empathic bond with that future self-image, they were able to overcome procrastination. The research also showed that it doesn't really matter whether a person is practicing mindfulness or visualization. Both are good ways of increasing that sense of connection to a future self.

When it comes to be beating procrastination, this research study shows that one of the best ways to visualize your future self is through a third-person perspective. Imagine you're watching a movie. Don't Imagine yourself in your own body and looking at it with your own eyes. This is a first-person perspective. Using a third-person perspective enables you to see the big picture and this level of connection can make you procrastinate less.

Chapter 15: Hang Out with Highly Motivated People Who Believe In Taking Action

Believe it or not, for every five friends you have, at least one person doesn't procrastinate. I know it sounds weird but, in any group of people, there's always a subgroup that have no problems with procrastination.

As the old saying goes, birds of a feather flock together. If you hang out with people who tend to procrastinate, don't be surprised if your own procrastination habits are reinforced by their presence. Just by hanging out with people, seeing how they work and their attitude, your tendency to procrastinate gets worse.

I'm not saying that you're necessarily dragging each other down, but you're definitely keeping each other in place. It's so much harder to break through and do what you need to do because there's really not much incentive as far as your social setting goes.

You only need to look around you and see that maybe you're overdoing things. Perhaps you're just stressing out too much so you're more likely to just kick the can down the road because, hey, everybody's doing it.

Peer Pressure is Real

I wish I could to tell you that if you hang out with people who procrastinate habitually, that them seeing you starting on time and ploughing through your tasks would motivate them to overcome procrastination. That kind of scenario is great for Hollywood movies but in real life, you're going to get a backlash.

I remember one of my first jobs out of college was in a government office. I was an unpaid intern and there were a lot of other unpaid interns from area colleges. It was a government office so, as you can imagine, the actual employees of that office were not exactly highly motivated. Most of them were just going through the motions. In fact, I could tell that a lot of them pretended to be busy. They looked busy but when you look at what they were actually doing and the impact of their work, they weren't actually doing much.

In that setting, it was very hard for me to produce because when I found myself in my own personal state of flow when I was just knocking one review after the other, a good friend of mine came up to me and said, "What are you doing? You're making us look bad. If this keeps up, you might set a new standard for productivity, and what do you think will happen to other people?" We both laughed at it and he tried to pass it off as a joke, but I got the message.

Peer pressure is real. People may not step up to you and tell you but there are certain unspoken rules. You have to abide by them.

This is why it's a good idea to hang out with motivated people who do not procrastinate. The good news is they're around you. They're in minority, but they are around. Find them. Hang out with those people.

Once you do, take lead roles on projects. Volunteer for projects and promise to timely deliver them. In that environment, social pressure will push you to not only start on time, but to get things done on time. Allow yourself to model yourself after these people.

A friend of mine told me that when he got out of college, he worked at this insurance company processing property damage claims. There's a lot involved in the work. The customer would come in. You fill out their paperwork, then you go out to the parking lot and look at their car. They open the hood or the trunk. You check the different parts and you write an estimate based on what you could see. You then come out, plug that into the computer, print it out and give them their copy, and off they go.

My friend was struggling through this whole process because it seemed that it had different moving parts. There were also a lot of things to memorize because the typical car is not exactly a simple piece of machinery. Depending on the damage on the car, you probably would have to remember at least a couple of dozen different parts.

He told me that the first nine months at that company, he rarely went home before 9:00 PM. This blew my mind because he would come in at 8:00 or 7:30, and he would stay all the way until 9:00.

He told me that he was doing a lot of experimentation. He would read a lot of books on car parts. He would have a checklist. He would listen to calming music. Nothing seemed to work.

He felt resigned to those long hours until he met Paul.

Paul was a senior claims adjuster who was assigned to my friend's office temporarily. Paul normally works out at the field.

The great thing about being a field adjuster is that you set your schedule. If you had five appointments that day, and you're able to knock them out in two hours, then you have yourself a two-hour work day. All the company cared about is whether you saw the vehicles that you were signed and that you filed the paper work that day. That's all they cared about.

Paul was a master of the one-hour workday. Can you imagine that? Seeing four to five cars in the span of an hour? He was kind of a legend in my friend's office.

My friend finally saw the man, the myth, the legend. It turned out to be all true. Paul would come in at 8:00 AM and, without fail, leave by 11:00 AM, if not earlier. In the first few weeks, my friend couldn't believe his eyes. He would just rub his eyes and say, "What just happened?" It's as if a human tornado came through the office and was quickly out the door right after my friend realized that it came in. What's going on?

He finally mustered up enough nerve to step up to Paul and ask him for a few tips. Paul was gracious enough to let my friend in on his secret. The secret was actually quite simple. It involved understanding what made you fearful or apprehensive about seeing damaged is cars, figuring out the parts involved, communicating it to the client, plugging all that information into an online form, and then printing it all out.

With that out of the way, Paul also taught my friend about visualization. He said, "It doesn't really matter how you do it. You can feel grateful. You can think of the times when you were actually able to work really fast for one call. However you do it, just do it and allow yourself to feel pumped up to knock out the next appointment as quickly as possible."

Soon enough, after hearing this advice and then seeing them practiced by Paul, my friend was able to start on time. He told me that this was quite a major breakthrough because one of the reasons he struggled with long hours is because he was constantly backlogged. He just can't, for the life of him, start on time.

When he did get started, things slowed down like molasses. What frustrated him was that not all his days were slow and unproductive. In some appointments, he would just zip through the appointment. It's as if everything fell into place. He was obviously describing his state of flow.

Paul agreed to time my friend and chart his actions. In the course of three weeks, my friend went from coming in at 7:30 to 8:00 in the morning and leaving at 9:00 or later to coming in at 8:00 AM and leaving at lunch time.

How was he able to it? He was able to beat procrastination. That was his problem all along.

He would procrastinate seeing the appointments as they come in; he would procrastinate plugging in the materials; and he would procrastinate filling out forms. It all seemed so complicated for him. He was so afraid of making a mistake that it dragged the whole process much longer than it needed to. In most cases, he was telling the customer that he would just mail them their copy of the estimate.

Paul enabled him to overcome his fear by holding his feet to the fire and acting as both a role model and as an accountability buddy, Paul was able to walk my friend through all the productivity techniques I have outlined in this book.

All the information I shared with you here is based on my friend's experience. It may not be the perfect case study, but it's good enough for you to build a framework with which you too can overcome procrastination.

Final Thoughts

I've got to warn you: while the information contained in this book absolutely works, it may not work for you. How come? You have to do them. You can't just think about them. You can't just read this book and feel good about all the insights and inspiration that you got.

While those are important, action is more important. This is why I need you to do me a big favor. I need you to start now. That's right. Drop everything that you're doing and start now.

You know that there's this one task that you'd rather avoid. In fact, you probably have been thinking about that task while you're reading this book. It's stuck in your mind, kind of like mental peanut butter. I want you to start on it now.

Please understand that if you don't start now and you're waiting for that "right time," you're just fooling yourself. You know full well that the right time will never come because there are just so many other things competing for your time and attention.

Don't fall into that trap. Stop giving yourself excuses to procrastinate on beating procrastination. As ridiculous as that sounds, that's exactly the game so many people play on themselves, and that's why they're stuck.

Stop basing your decisions on your feelings. You can feel crappy. That's okay. You still need to start. You can feel good, and that's awesome. You need to start. Just start today.

Once you start, you have to commit to keep going. The first few times, it's going to be murder. You're not used to it. The other things that you feel that you want to do seem so tempting; but after you apply the techniques I've shared with you in this book, you start gaining momentum. It becomes easier and easier.

My advice then is to level up. I'm not just talking about to keep on moving. I'm talking about leveling up. Challenge yourself more. That's how you grow.

I wish you nothing but awesome success in your future. Believe me, beating procrastination is definitely one key milestone to the success you want.

Copyright © Nicholas Mayor 2019

All rights to this book are reserved. No permission is given for any part of this book to be reproduced, transmitted in any form or means; electronic or mechanical, stored in a retrieval system, photocopied, recorded, scanned, or otherwise. Any of these actions require the proper written permission of the publisher.

Disclaimer

All erudition contained in this book is given for informational and educational purposes only. The author is not in any way accountable for any results or outcomes that emanate from using this material. Constructive attempts have been made to provide information that is both accurate and effective, but the author is not bound for the accuracy or use/misuse of this information.

www.ingramcontent.com/pod-product-compliance
Lightning Source LLC
Chambersburg PA
CBHW022101170526
45157CB00004B/1438